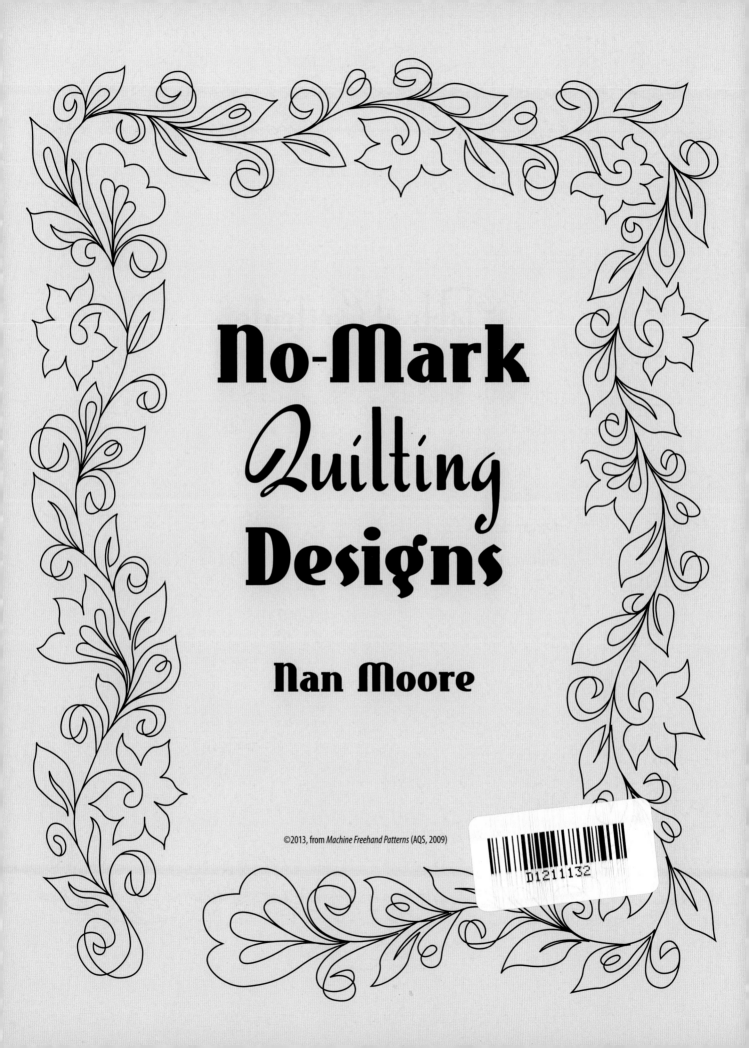

# No-Mark
# Quilting
# Designs

## Nan Moore

# Table of Contents

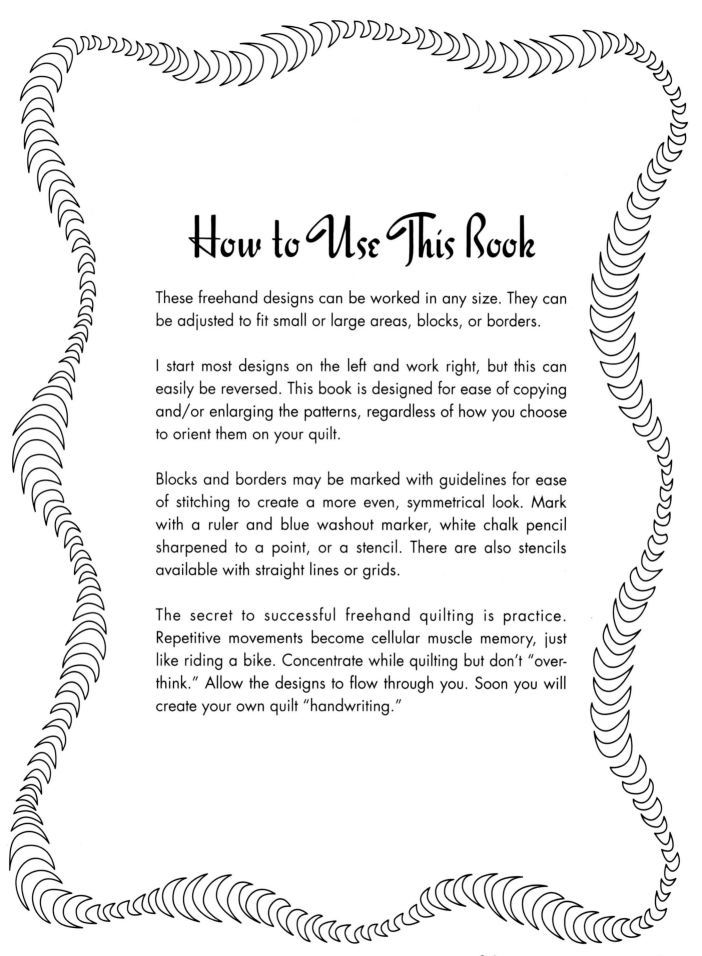

# How to Use This Book

These freehand designs can be worked in any size. They can be adjusted to fit small or large areas, blocks, or borders.

I start most designs on the left and work right, but this can easily be reversed. This book is designed for ease of copying and/or enlarging the patterns, regardless of how you choose to orient them on your quilt.

Blocks and borders may be marked with guidelines for ease of stitching to create a more even, symmetrical look. Mark with a ruler and blue washout marker, white chalk pencil sharpened to a point, or a stencil. There are also stencils available with straight lines or grids.

The secret to successful freehand quilting is practice. Repetitive movements become cellular muscle memory, just like riding a bike. Concentrate while quilting but don't "overthink." Allow the designs to flow through you. Soon you will create your own quilt "handwriting."

# Basics

Machine quilting is just like pencil doodling, but with thread.

Start with a line, make a shape, then repeat that shape in a continuous pattern.

Using basic shapes, you can add to and change a meander in endless variations.

A flower can be as simple as two circles.

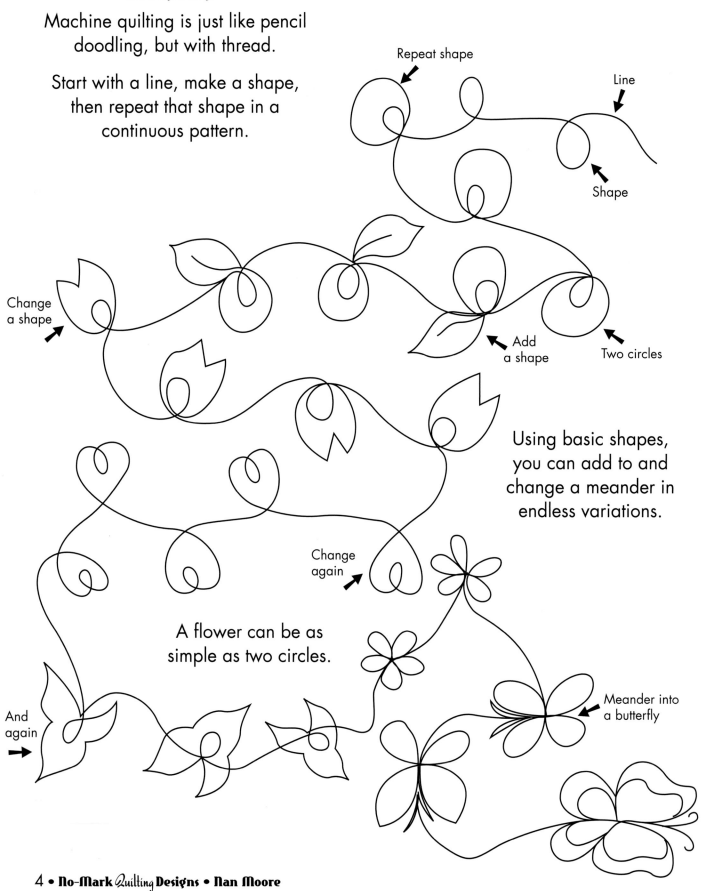

Repeat shape

Line

Shape

Change a shape

Add a shape

Two circles

Change again

Meander into a butterfly

And again

# Changing Direction

# Let the Motion Evolve

Watch this swirl action develop...

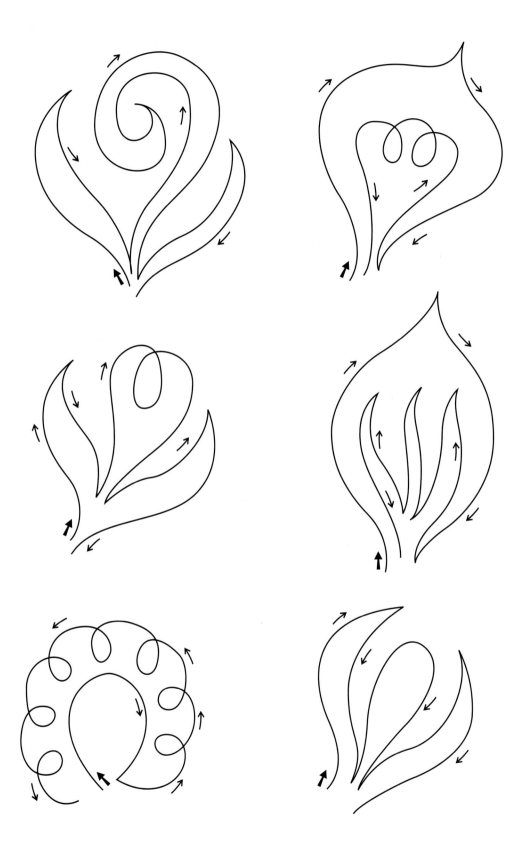

and change...

and become more elaborate.

$\mathcal{Size}$   Leaf and swirl designs can be stitched small or large.

# Meanders

# Leaves

Leaves come in various shapes and can be used in many quilting designs. There are three basic leaf shapes:

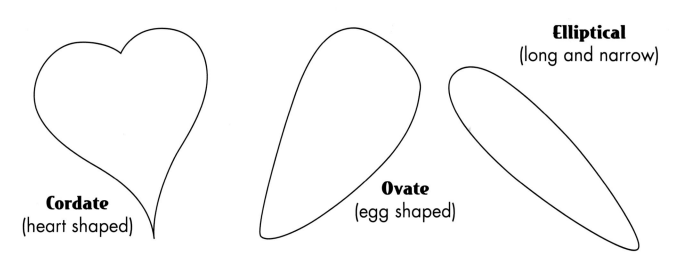

**Cordate**
(heart shaped)

**Ovate**
(egg shaped)

**Elliptical**
(long and narrow)

Practice drawing shapes, then add stems and turn them into leaves.

# Leafy Variations I

# Leafy Variations II

# Leaf and Swirl (around appliqué)

Appliqué

# Flowers - Simple to Fancy

**Clover**

**Simple Feather Leaf**

**Fishies**

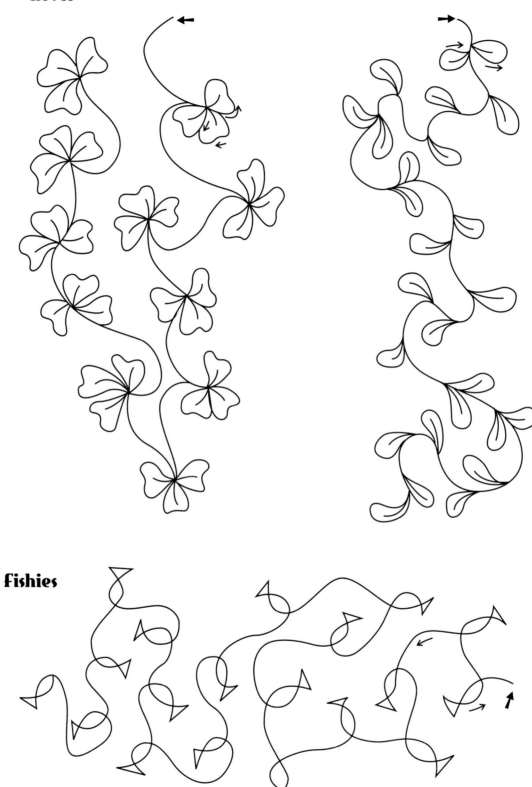

# Heart Variations

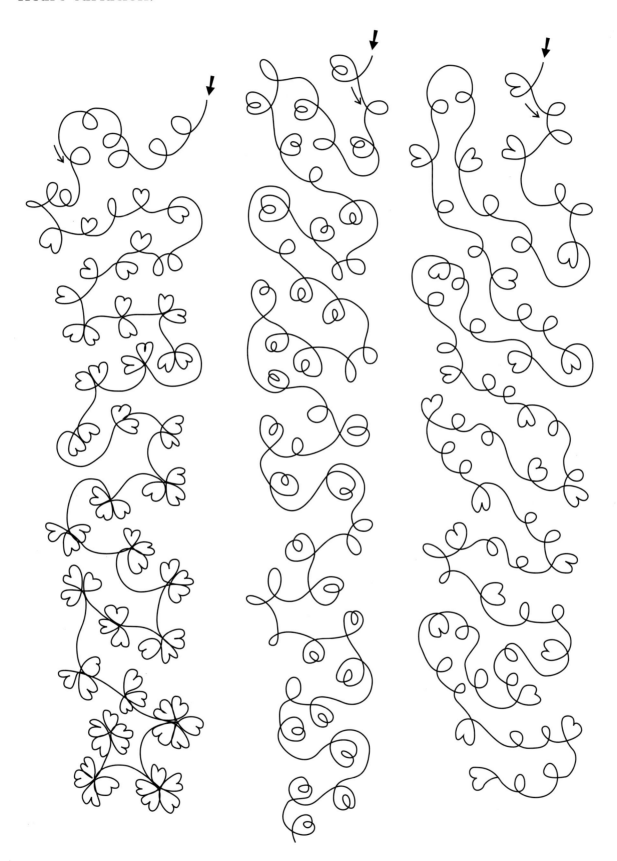

**One-Way Loops**

**Jacobean Meander**

**Button Flower**

## Simple Rose

## Holly Leaves

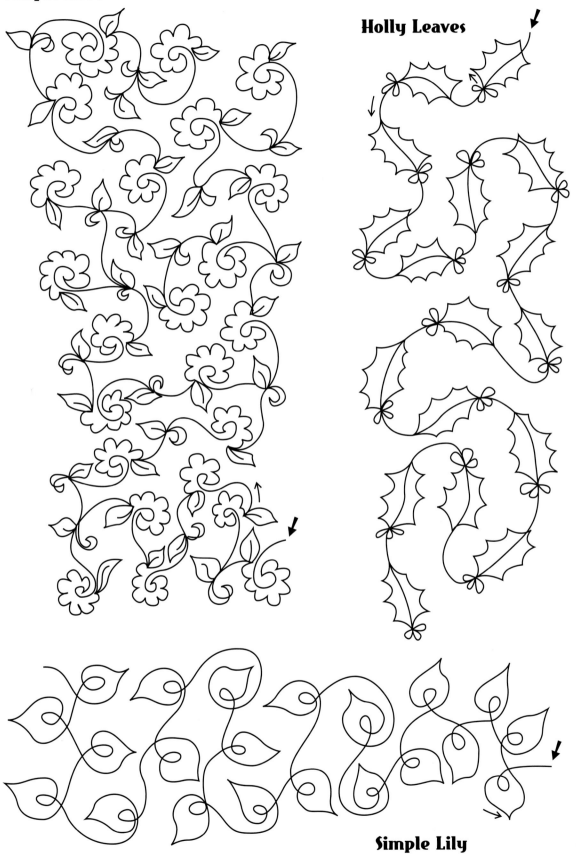

## Simple Lily

## Columbine with Buds

## Dancing Dahlia

## Double Heart Flower

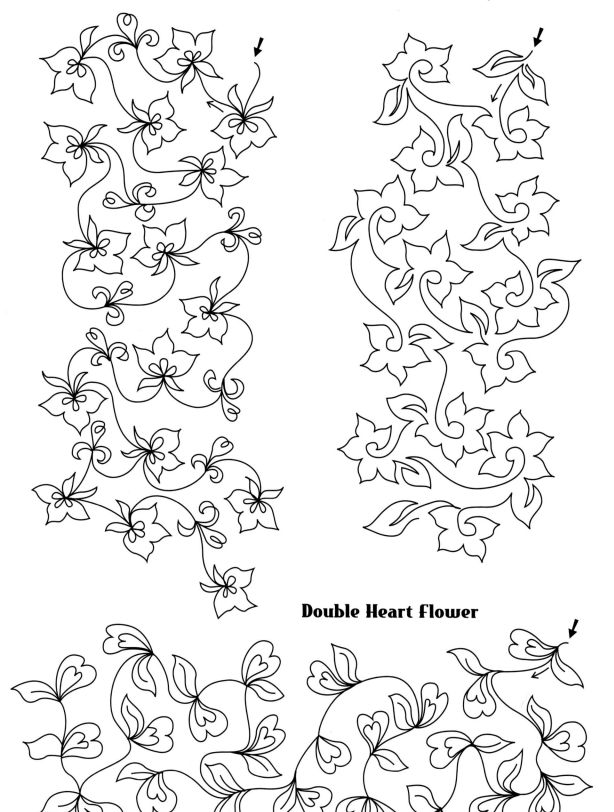

# Butterflies and Bees

# Dragonfly How-to

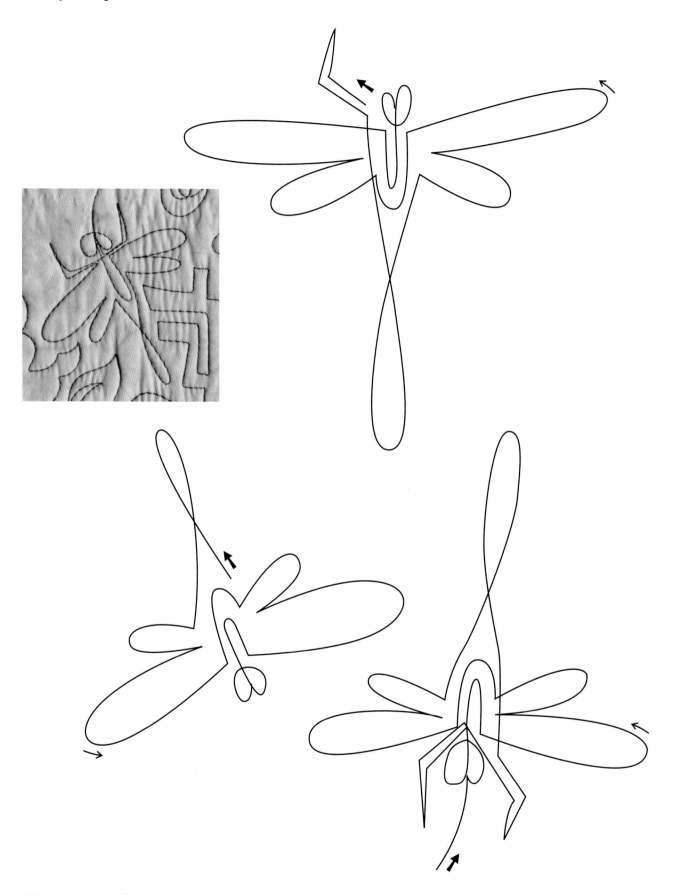

# Allovers

# Bump Oak Leaves

# Simple Maple Leaves

# Veined Maple Leaves

## Willow Leaves